Cat Coloring Book

An Adult Coloring Book for Cat Lovers

CREATIVE COLORING PRESS

CATS

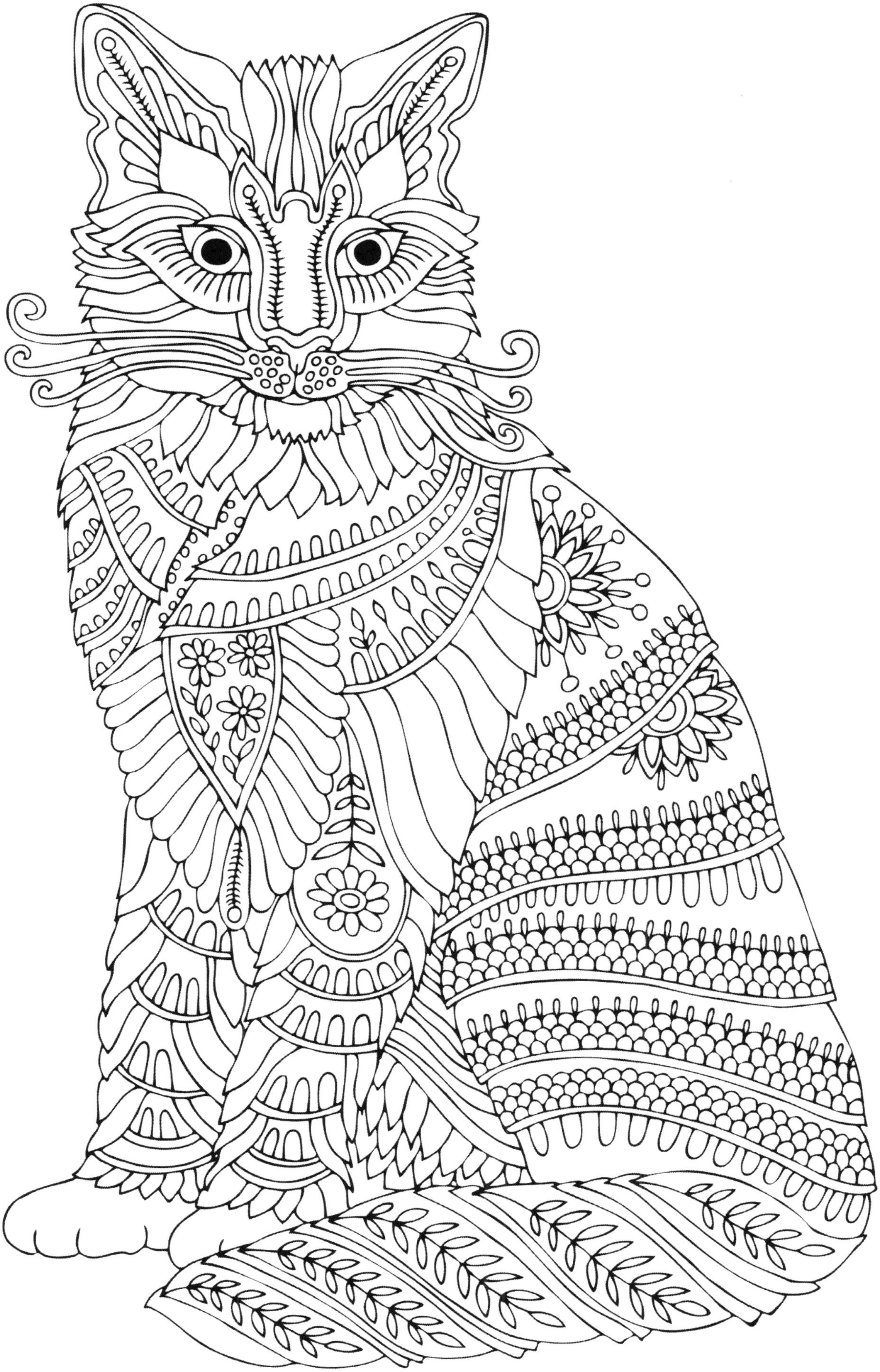

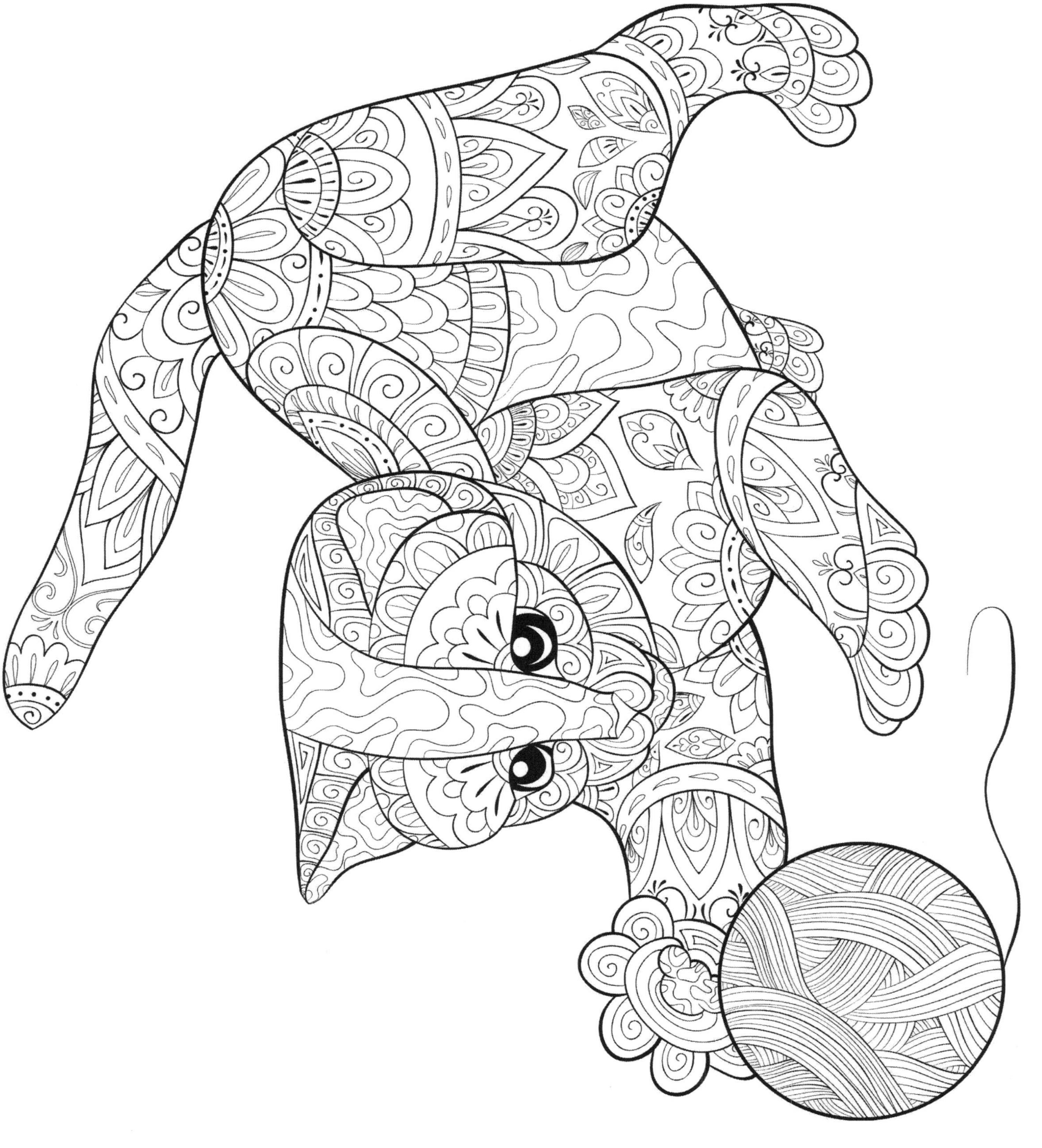

1985
MAUST
Mrs Halloway
The Scarlet Matter
The Color Pink
Robin Food
The Catcher of the Pie
Diary
King Tear
Brave New Purr
The Great Catsby
Lord of the Mice
E = mc²
The Silence of the Dogs
Alice in Slumber-Land
Song of Salmon
1001 Days
Paradise
Eat Pray Purr
Kitten Love
Cat Photography
Albert Catmus
Franz Katzka
Gone with the Mint
Catbeth
A Tale of Two Cats
Poetry
Lord of the Flings
Flowers
Art
A Midwinter Day's Dream
50 Shades of Meow
Life of Pie
The Phantom of the Theater
The Chronicles of Tortilla
Recipes
Cake
The Catfathe

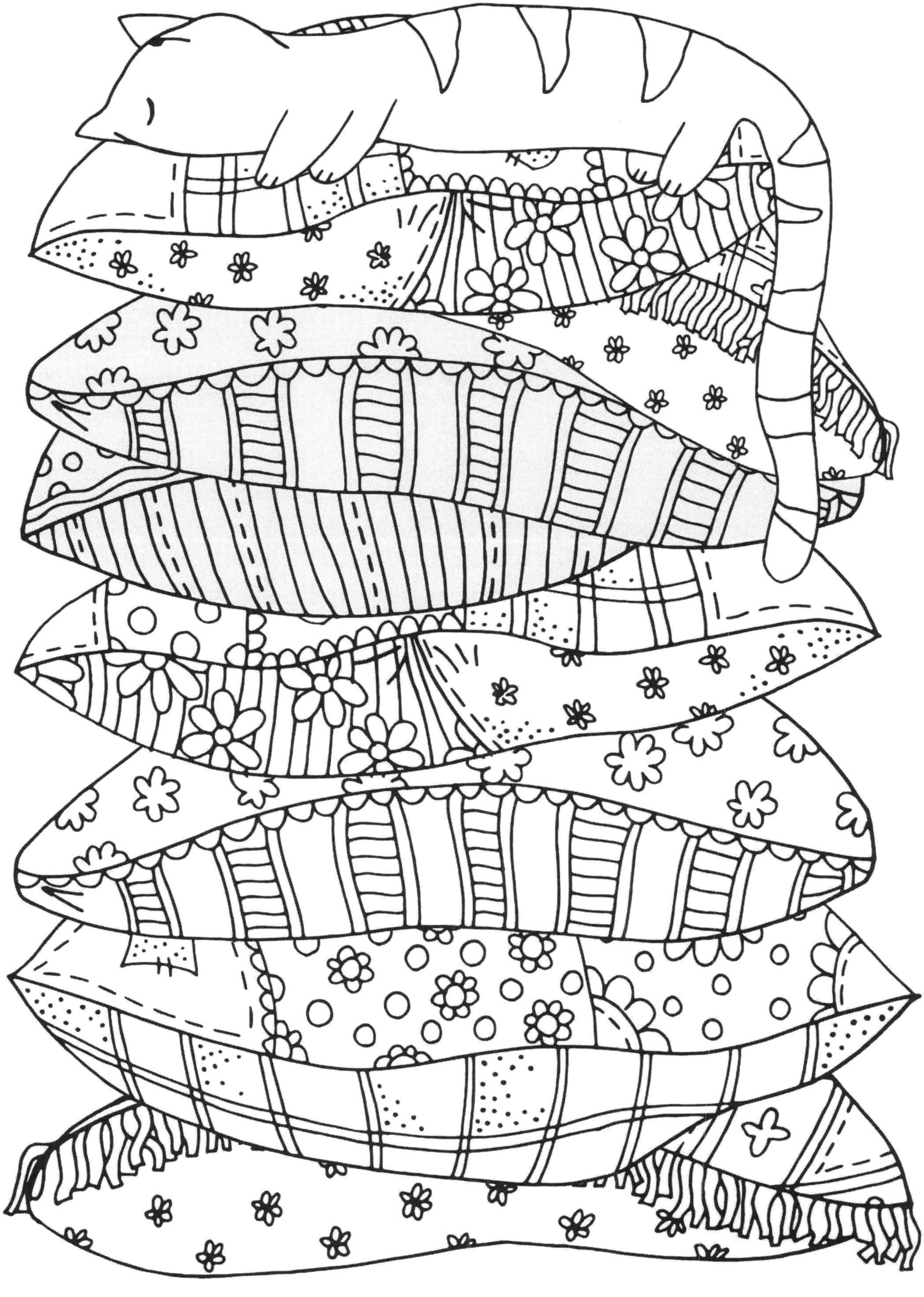

First edition: 2018

Photo credits: Shutterstock